Transition

On

Purpose.

Self-Reflect, Explore and Re-Engage Life

Dennis J. Volpe, CDR, USN (Retired)

Endorsements:

"Transition on Purpose is a very personal story about resilience.   The personal leadership lessons will lead to tremendous positive change in both your professional and personal life! Dennis' Transition on Purpose framework will change how you think, how you behave, and how you act!"

~•Melissa Twiningdavis, President, Precision Castparts Corporation, Small Castings, IGT, Technologies

"Having started more than a dozen companies over the past 4-decades has taught me that we are in constant transition. I would suggest strongly that you listen to the wisdom of Dennis Volpe in his amazing compilation of life experiences in his new release, *Transition On Purpose.* He teaches us to live proactively, not reactively."

~ Aaron T. Walker, *View From The Top*

"In *Transition on Purpose,* Dennis has done an excellent job of showing personal leadership and resilience principles in action with a very personal and impactful story. His story shows us what living a resilient life can look like and feel like. His insight and down-to-earth perspective will leave you better equipped to bring out the best in yourself and those around you."

~ **Jennifer H. Selke, Ph.D.**

Director of Veteran Programs & Campus Outcomes

Camp Southern Ground

"Dennis blends his passion for personal leadership and his extensive firsthand knowledge of resilience to deliver an insightful, compelling and instructional read. His personal leadership concepts are straightforward, easy to understand, and applicable to so many audiences. *Transition on Purpose* will leave you better equipped to live your life more intentionally."

~ **Howard Morgan**

Author and Co-Founder of Top 50 Coaches

"Dennis presents a very personal transition story full of journeys in emotional intelligence, resilience and decision making. *Transition on Purpose* provides a comprehensive and straightforward personal leadership methodology to utilize as you navigate the transitions in your own life."

~ Dr. Derek Mann, Phd
Associate Professor and Health and Human Performance Coach
Jacksonville University

Table of Contents

Endorsements: 7

Introduction   13

Learning About Transition   19

A Crucible   23

Search Inward: Hard Learning   29

The Man in the Mirror   35

Explore Outward - The Process   41

  Swim, Bike, Run   45

  Health, People, and Purpose   55

  Mentorship   59

  Alignment   63

  Frameworks Make the Mind Work   65

  Life Happens For You   69

Action: The Program   79

What's the Objective?   83

Know Your Values   87

Identify and Accept your Reality   93

Illuminate Your "WHY"   99

Embrace Your Constraints and Restraints 103

Crystalize Your Priorities 107

Build Your Network 111

    Your Quick Reaction Force (QRF) 113

    Your Tribe 117

    Masterminds 121

Equip Your Transition Toolkit 125

Develop a Plan & Know It'll Change 129

The After-Action Report (AAR) 135

Thank you 137

What are the nine secrets to get us there? 139

The Man in the Arena 141

LET'S CONNECT 143

Introduction

"The longest and the shortest life, then, amount to the same, for the present moment lasts the same for all and is all anyone possesses. No one can lose either the past or the future, for how can someone be deprived of what's not theirs."

- Marcus Aurelius

Adversity is a natural part of the human condition. Life is going to give you challenges, obstacles, and most importantly, opportunities. When we are given those opportunities, we are going to transition on purpose, by accident, or by force. I've experienced all three types of transition.

It is up to us to determine our personal definition of transition. Transitioning on purpose is about self-reflection, exploration, connection, and action. It's taking the time to understand who we are, what really matters to us and why, exploring those ideas, connecting with the people in our lives who can assist in our journey, and creating opportunities and options to take deliberate and focused action.

Transitioning on accident is the exact opposite. It is a passive acceptance rather than taking informed and deliberate action towards a defined goal.

Forced transition is being forced out of what you want to do, unwillingly, and having to find another purpose. This can be either an evolutionary process that happens over time or a revolutionary experience that is precipitated by a singular event.

In hindsight, I really ended up transitioning into a military career by accident. When it was time to decide to stay in the Navy or do something different, the Navy provided answers to the questions I didn't know I needed to be asking myself regarding more pay, education, and more time with family and friends.

The Navy made my career transition decision quite simple and there was little effort on my part to sign on the dotted line and say yes. No self-reflection, limited   exploration, and a little bit of action in terms of my signature on some paperwork — that was my initial transition into a military career as a Naval officer.

This book will provide my personal story as well as a framework you can consider to guide you to think differently about your future personal and professional transitions.

This framework, called *Transition on Purpose*, was informed by the work of Dr. Terrence Maltbia of the Columbia University Coaching Certification Program. The Columbia Coaching model provides the backbone, while my personal experiences, education, and professional coaching engagements have informed the action steps.

As you move forward, **S**earching Inward, **E**xploring Outward, and **A**ction will be part of your decision-making process and transition planning. If you want to figure out where you are going, you need to go to SEA.

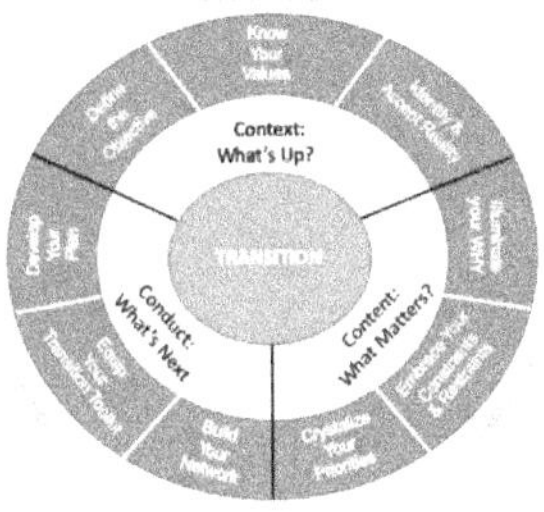

Reproduced with permission from: The Columbia Coaching Program (Internal or External). Dr. Terrence Maltbia, Faculty Director. New York, New York, Columbia University.

Learning About Transition

"What is to change a person is to change his awareness of himself."
- Abraham Maslow

My first transition, committing to a career as a Naval Officer, was completely by accident. I never intended to make the military a career, but I wanted to take advantage of the opportunities a service academy education and military experience offered in terms of life and leadership experiences, service to my country and everything that went with that.

When my initial military service obligation was ending, I had not put much thought into what I wanted my next chapter to look like because I knew I wanted to go into federal law enforcement. My father was a retired police officer and I knew a lot of Naval

Academy graduates who went into a federal law enforcement career after their service obligations, so it just made sense to me. Service to country and community was something that was instilled in me at a very young age and a follow-on federal law enforcement career would enable me to continue serving others. However, in early 2001, there was a federal hiring freeze, so the one option I had only slightly thought about was no longer an option.

As luck would have it, the Navy had a more detailed plan and provided me with an ideal solution — an opportunity to pursue a graduate degree in leadership development and spend additional time at the United States Naval Academy teaching leadership in the morning and coaching rugby in the afternoons. Life was good.

And then, September 11, 2001, happened. A day that changed my life and lives of so many Americans forever. It was a day that thrust the American military into war for at least the next two decades and made my "non-decision" that much easier to make.

Before I realized it, I had signed up for four more years in the Navy and followed an accidental transition into a military career because it aligned with my commitment to service, it was low risk, and I didn't really have to think about it. It was the easy button.

Fortunately, this accidental transition early in my career sparked a passion and purpose in my heart that would shape my future endeavors. I have a passion for empowering others to live their best lives. Part of that process is being able to enlighten others to accept their current reality, to define their desired end state, and equip them with the tools and resources they need to get there — to transition on purpose.

Today, I have a successful career in executive performance and transition coaching and leadership development consulting that provides the autonomy I need in order to make the impact I want at both the organizational and individual level. It provides me the opportunity to spend time with the people and organizations that matter, do the work that is impactful for others, and be able to positively impact my community and the lives of those in it. My coaching and leadership consulting career provides some of the same sense of purpose I had when I was a military officer.

A Crucible

Success is to be measured not so much by the position that one has reached in life as by the obstacles which he has overcome.

- Booker T. Washington

On the evening of February 11, 2014, I found myself on the bridge wing of a guided missile frigate on a national tasking maritime security mission in support of the 2014 Winter Olympics off the coast of Sochi, Russia.

The ship was close enough we could see the Olympic torch in the foreground of the Sochi mountains. It was close enough that we had the opportunity to interact with multiple Russian maritime security assets and our actions were being briefed to the highest levels of U.S. military and civilian leadership.

In the blink of an eye - I had gone from instructor duty in Annapolis, Maryland, through two highly successful Department Heads tours, another graduate degree program at the Naval War College, a year-long operational planner tour in Afghanistan, and an Executive Officer tour with a counter-piracy deployment to the Horn of Africa and was now commanding an American warship at sea during forward deployed operations. I was literally on top of the world — conducting a national level tasking mission, providing maritime security for the Olympics, and leading a crew of exceptional Officers and Sailors. For a ship captain, it really couldn't get much better than that.

Up to that point, I had been myopically focused on my unplanned military career and doing the best I could. Twenty-four hours a

day, seven days a week, 365 days a year —
that was how I was taught and that was the
expectation, or, at least, my assumption of the
expectation. For an unplanned career, being
selected to command a warship at sea was a
pretty good deal and it placed me in the
company of some dedicated and impressive
professional military officers. However,
along the way, I lost focus on nearly every
other aspect of my life.

That evening, we checked off station,
departed our maritime security patrol area,
and headed across the Black Sea over to
Samsun, Turkey. The intent was to conduct
what we referred to as a brief stop for fuel and
supplies, or a "BSF," so we could get back
"on station" and continue our maritime
security duties for another week.

It was the morning of February 12, 2014. The sun was out, there was a nice sea breeze and we were on schedule for our port visit. Everything was moving in the right direction — until it wasn't.

As we were heading into the harbor, my ship ran aground at the entrance of Samsun harbor, 50 yards north of the center of the channel. Three propeller blades were damaged and the ship was deemed non-mission capable during a time of heightened tensions in the Black Sea region. In the span of 24 hours, I went from being on top of the world to being in the loneliest valley for a professional military officer — complete mission failure. My ship, my team, my responsibility.

After a brief investigation, I was justly relieved of my duties because a Commanding

Officer is always 100% responsible and accountable for the actions or inactions of his or her command and the members therein. I readily accepted and owned that responsibility when I assumed command on November 13, 2012, and said the words "I relieve you, sir." Those words, followed by the words "I stand relieved," while simple and straightforward, take the burden of command, the complete responsibility and accountability for a warship and the Officers and Sailors that give it life, off of the shoulders of one person and place it squarely on another. The events of February 12, 2014, were my burden to bear and mine alone.

What I was not completely prepared for was the military judicial process and the forced transition that would be my reality over the next two years.

Search Inward: Hard Learning

"If a man knows not to which port he sails, no wind is favorable."

- Seneca

As you may have realized by now, my story isn't neat-and-tidy. It provides examples of success, failure, resilience, and opportunity and offers lessons you can leverage instead of having to make that journey yourself. When you don't take the time to sort out what really matters to you there is a good chance you can end up in a profession where your role and your identity overlap. More simply, what you do is who you are and who you are is what you do.

In the Navy, especially as an Officer, you are rarely referred to by your name. You are known and referred to by your job — Commo

(Communications Officer), First (First Lieutenant), Weps (Weapons Officer), CSO (Combat Systems Officer), XO (Executive Officer), and then Captain.

Once in command, especially in the Surface Navy, you are known by your ship's namesake. Coming to work, leaving work, and even on the radio, "Ding, Ding . . . Ding, Ding – TAYLOR arriving." "Ding, Ding . . . Ding, Ding – TAYLOR departing." "This is PROUD DEFENDER, roger, over." In a military organization, especially in command, it is easy to forget who you are because you become so invested and committed to the success of the unit, the command, the organization, and those dedicated to mission success. "Mission First, Sailors Always." That was my reality.

Unfortunately, the organization from

which I had drawn my identity for 22 years and had inscribed my name on the side of the Navy Memorial in Washington, D.C. for outstanding operational excellence would later say, "You know what? You're never going to have the opportunity to be in command again." And then worse, "We don't even know if you should be part of this organization moving forward." It leaves an imprint on your soul. You have to figure out who you are, what really matters to you, why it matters to you, and what's next.

The impact my new reality had on me physically, mentally, emotionally, and socially was not something I expected. I experienced headaches, difficulty concentrating on things and random mood swings due to the stress of the military judicial process, followed by a process to determine whether or not I should even be allowed to stay in the Naval Service. Everything that was a part of who I was, was now in question. I questioned myself and my abilities. I stopped trusting my inner voice to make decisions. I tried to compartmentalize my emotions of grief, shame, fear, and anger in order to move forward in a positive direction. I learned pretty quickly who I could really trust, confide in and rely on.

Trying to hike out of that lonely valley — the start of my forced transition from military service — would require grit and resilience. Not because I couldn't continue serving in the Navy but, because of the military judicial process and the impact on my career, I would not be able to serve in a way that made sense for me — to command Officers and Sailors at sea.

Everything that I'd done up to that point in my life was now open to question and interpretation, both internally and everywhere I looked externally. I doubted myself, both personally and professionally, because the identity I had known for over 20 years had been stripped away. I needed to figure out who I was, what really mattered to me, and what I stood for. I now had the opportunity to reach down into my own human psyche — a pretty scary place if you had never been there. And I really hadn't.

The Man in the Mirror

"No person is free who is not a master of himself."

- Epictetus

Part of any transition equation is resilience — the ability to recover from or adjust easily to adversity, misfortune, or change and move in a positive and productive direction. For me, it was all of that and more.

You truly can't appreciate the impact a crucible experience will have on you physically, mentally, or socially until it happens. So how can you make sure you are prepared for a personal or professional crucible moment and truly know how to transition on purpose? You need to go back to SEA. Funny, since that's where my unplanned military career unraveled for my betterment.

"Between stimulus and response there is a space. In that space is our power to choose our response. In our response lies our growth and our freedom."

- Victor Frankl

In terms of purpose and passion, it's not until you do some intentional self-reflection, real head-work and heart-work — that bumpy highway between our brain and our heart that we really don't like to travel down — that you're going to transition from where you are to where you want to go with purpose. Change is inevitable. Change is what happens to us. Transition is an internal process - mindset shift - and really what happens for us to move in a positive and productive direction.

I realized it wasn't just about being a Naval Officer. My "why" was more about positively impacting the lives of others. I wanted to have significance in my life and to be known for my commitment to making the lives of other people better. It was my professional misfortune — having a bad day at sea — and the events that followed, that empowered me to endure, to really understand and embrace personal and professional resilience and to move in a positive direction.

The whole concept of support, connection, and accountability as part of a transition process cannot be overemphasized. I have been blessed beyond measure to have a loving wife who provided amazing support, counsel, and encouragement throughout my journey, even when I refused to open up about where I was and how the journey was impacting me. Her support, combined with the trusted connection to one of the most nonjudgmental and stoic dogs around, provided a very stable platform to launch from.

Couple that with the support, connection, and positive energy from amazing family, friends, and colleagues I met during my transition journey, and the foundation was set to move in a positive direction. Surround yourself with supportive and positive people and you will be amazed at what you can accomplish. The only way to change the world is to start in your own backyard with people who are passionate, positive, courageous, and committed to your success.

So, how do we need to think about personal change management? I was fortunate to attend the Professional Science (PROSCI) Change Management course where I learned personal change management is about managing awareness and desire. Why do we stay where we are? Because it's easy. Because it's comfortable. Because it doesn't take much effort. How do you get the desire to change? By seeing the value of the transition and embracing the fact that the energy and time required to get to where we want to go is much less than the happiness and fulfillment we will have once we get to where we want to be.

Are you going to embrace the suck each and every day just because that's what you've been doing? Or are you going to take the time to figure out, "You know what? This is what I value. This is what matters to me. This is what I want to prioritize and the energy and effort required to get me there is worth it because I don't want to stay and sit with the status quo."

The first step is self-reflection — to accept reality, to identify what matters and prioritize what's important. The next step is exploration - sorting out options and opportunities. The final step is Action - building your Tribe, developing a plan and getting after it.

Explore Outward - The Process

*"Dig deep within yourself, for there is a fountain of
goodness ever ready to flow if you will keep
digging."*

- Marcus Aurelius

During my transition, I had the opportunity to participate in several unique programs and experiences that aided in my personal development and transition journey. I want to share them with you for a few reasons. First, there are a lot of organizations out there dedicated to supporting your journey and it's up to you to sort out which make the most sense for you. Second, you will be pleasantly surprised by what you learn about yourself, about others, and about life as long as you are open to the process and curious about the possibilities. Third, the combination of these unique experiences provided some of the resources I needed to put me on an awesome trajectory to do what I really wanted to do.

The first program was Operation New Uniform in Jacksonville, Florida. It is a comprehensive military transition program purposely designed to challenge one's old way of thinking and promote self-reflection to identify new pathways, new connections, and new opportunities.

As you can imagine, voluntarily going to a non-mandatory transition program designed to challenge my thinking and encourage self-reflection was not something I was really interested in doing. However, the support of the Operation New Uniform team was amazing and they opened my eyes to a lot of things that I knew were going on but refused to admit to myself or others.

The first big takeaway from my ONU experience was the realization that I had a role versus identity problem that had yet to be resolved. The second was that I needed to expand and strengthen both my personal and professional network in order to move in a positive direction. Both would take a long time to sort out and get right.

Swim, Bike, Run

As the events of February 12, 2014, were investigated, written about, blogged about, and finally adjudicated, my personal fortitude and hardiness were tested on a regular basis. I was fortunate enough to have a mentor tell me "get focused on something for yourself, otherwise this process will consume all of you." He was absolutely right.

Some days it truly did, but most days I did not let it because I began to understand, appreciate, and embrace what it meant to live a resilient life — one that recovers from and responds to adversity in a constructive and positive manner. My personal definition of resilience has evolved over time, but, in general, one's resiliency factor incorporates a commitment to meaningful goals, a constant connection to one's personal ethos, a realistic sense of one's reality, and the engagement of supportive and positive people.

With those factors in mind, the next path of my journey was becoming an aspiring triathlete, which, much to my surprise, provided me with my current understanding and appreciation of personal resilience, what is required to have it, and why it's an integral part of any transition. Mind, body, tribe, and why.

The sport of triathlon comprises three separate events — the swim, the bike, and the run — with a transition between each event. There are different triathlon events based on distance, commonly referred to as a Sprint, an

Olympic, a Half, or 70.3, and a Full, or 140.6. Each challenges you in a different way, both mentally and physically.

So, how does my career transition relate to being a triathlete? In order to distract myself from my current reality, and without much thought, planning, or conversation, I signed up for a Half-Ironman 70.3 event, which is a 1.2-mile swim, a 56-mile bike, and a 13.1-mile run.

It was only after I signed up that I realized a few important things. First, I had not done any real distance swimming since my junior year at the Naval Academy 19 years prior. Second, I wasn't even a good swimmer 19 years earlier. Third, I didn't even own a real road bike, much less a triathlon-equipped bike, and I could not even remember the last time I was on anything other than a beach cruiser or a mountain bike. The only thing I had going for me was that throughout my military career running was something I enjoyed. I had completed a couple of full marathons and a bunch of half marathons, so that part of the triathlon equation seemed doable. It might even be helpful to mention that I am not the ideal triathlon body archetype either. My swim coach told me I either needed to be four inches taller or needed to increase my wingspan by a few more inches to even think of being efficient in the water. Heck, I can remember standing in line to register for Ironman North Carolina with a USA Rugby t-shirt on and I had someone, who was the ideal triathlon body archetype, say, "Hmm, you are not built like most triathletes." I took a second to think about what he said, looked down at my USA Rugby t-shirt, and politely responded, "Yes, sir, I would absolutely agree but I'll get this finished. You don't look much like a Rugby player. Have you ever played or would you like to?" I never got an answer, but I did finish Ironman North Carolina.

The time required for the multi-sport lifestyle cemented emotional self-awareness lessons, the most important of which was how to respond to the changes in my life and the lives of those around me. Many friends, family, and co-workers were surprised by my optimism during my transition, but the multi-sport lifestyle — swimming, cycling, and running, sometimes up to 20 hours per week — provided the time necessary for the self-reflection and exploration I needed to sort things out. My identity had always been rolled into my profession, which was being chipped away bit by bit, and I needed to figure out what really mattered to me. More simply, I wanted to be the best version of myself and truly committed to positively impacting the lives of those around me. It was the commitment to my personal "why" that enlightened and empowered me to maintain a positive outlook and get things done. If you ever need to figure some stuff out in life, train for a Half-Ironman or an Ironman.

Understanding my strengths and maximizing them while appreciating my weaknesses was a key lesson from my triathlon journey. Swimming — a weakness. Biking — an opportunity. Running — a strength.

I spent enough time in the pool and took some lessons from a professional swim coach to not be a risk to myself and others. I capitalized on the biking opportunity and focused on running. The result was feeling confident for my first 70.3 — the very self-confidence I had lost during the previous months.

The other unexpected result was my own personal triathlon tribe — a group of amazingly supportive family and friends who were already established triathletes in their own right or who just got into the sport. This tribe is one I am still connected with today and they continue to provide the connection, energy, comedy relief, and accountability I need on a regular basis.

My triathlon journey from the Miami Half-Ironman 70.3 in 2014 to Ironman North Carolina 140.6 in 2016 involved several sprint distance triathlons, a few Olympic distance events, and a handful of 70.3 events. The experience provided a four-pronged approach of disciplined focus:

Mental Health & Mindfulness: Developing a regular routine to gain a sense of clarity in order to focus on what's important.

Physical Health & Wellness: Developing a sustainable physical wellness routine that promoted emotional and mental strength while enabling the function and mobility I wanted in my life.

Tribe: Developing a strong personal network which provided positive energy, a sense of connection, and accountability.

Why: Developing a strong sense and connection to what I wanted to do in the future and the motivations for that direction.

This solution set provided the self-control necessary to keep most of my negative self-perception at a manageable distance and enabled me to have a better appreciation for the controllable and uncontrollable aspects of life. I now consider it my resiliency toolkit.

Life happens and personal crucibles can happen to anyone at any time, so taking the time to understand and appreciate the controllable and uncontrollable aspects of one's life is extremely important. Being able to provide context to yourself and others and focus your energy and time on those controllable aspects and on what truly matters, will provide much more control and personal fulfillment. Surrounding yourself with supportive and positive people is a main ingredient in the "secret sauce" to increasing your capacity to re-engage life.

Health, People, and Purpose

Team Red, White, and Blue (RWB) and the Eagle Leader Fellow program provided an awesome opportunity to focus on my physical and emotional health by being around people who were committed to bettering themselves and their communities through physical activity and social interaction. Additionally, the people I was able to interact with provided a renewed sense of purpose in my life.

Much to my surprise, my Team RWB journey actually started back in Annapolis, Maryland, when I was a Leadership Instructor trying to decide if a military career even made sense for me. At the time, the

Naval Academy Athletic Program encouraged its student athletes to invite their favorite instructors to provide pre-game motivation talks and I was invited to give one to the varsity women's soccer team prior to one of their home games.

Fast forward over 11 years later and the Chapter Captain for Team RWB Jacksonville just happened to be one of those soccer players that had been in that locker room. I'm not even sure what I said that day, but I guess it was impactful enough for her to remember me and ask me to be part of the Team RWB Jacksonville Leadership Team. This would eventually lead to me being the Chapter Captain and then an Eagle Leader Fellow for the Southeast Region of Team RWB.

My sense of purpose came from having the opportunity to lead the Jacksonville, Florida, chapter of Team RWB and positively impact the lives of military veterans and civilians alike. The awesome byproduct of my Team RWB experience has been the connection with some of the most caring, selfless, and personable people I have ever met and who are part of my personal tribe to this day.

Mentorship

The American Corporate Partners (ACP) Veteran Mentor Program was an amazing year-long transition experience which provided the opportunity to interact with a mentor who was completely invested in my success. Mentorship is about providing others guidance and direction based on one's experience and expertise to equip them for future learning and growth opportunities. I was privileged to have a mentor who took the time and invested their energy to enable me to illuminate what truly mattered to me and develop a plan to get there.

I met with my mentor every few weeks and we explored some of the deeper life questions and some simple ones I hadn't really considered before like, "What's really going to make you happy?" Or "What do you really want to prioritize moving forward?" The most important parts of the interaction were the exploratory questions, the contextual reality, and the space my mentor provided me to explore the answers to those questions and how they would fit into my new reality. We were able to explore where I wanted to go, why I wanted to go there, and what made the most sense for me based on my skill set, my experiences, and my passion to enlighten, empower, and equip others for success.

The key takeaways from that experience were the need for professional networking and the realization that it was OK to ask for help. I learned that asking for help wasn't a sign of weakness, but one of personal strength and courage.

My ACP experience had a profound impact and instilled a desire to pay things forward. Being an ACP Veteran Transition Mentor is now part of my personal "why" and it is something that provides a sense of purpose, connection, and personal fulfillment.

Alignment

The first transition game changer was finding an organization to work with that aligned with my personal values. Zig Ziglar is quoted as saying, "Success occurs when opportunity meets preparation." My initial transition success came from two seemingly random lunch conversations that epitomize the importance of developing a strong personal and professional network. Those initial conversations led to additional discussions about next steps and working with the Leadership Research Institute as a leadership and organizational development consultant and coach.

Why was this a game changer? I found an organization that provided me with the autonomy I was looking for and the opportunity to positively impact the lives and careers of others.

But why was it really helpful to me?

I found an organization and a team of recognized leadership professionals who had more confidence in me and my abilities than I did in myself at that point in my transition. The mentorship and opportunities I was provided started a much needed personal resilience renewal process that has equipped me with the tools necessary to enlighten and empower others and equip them with the tools they need to succeed.

Frameworks Make the Mind Work

The next stop in my journey was the Columbia University Executive Coaching Certification program. This program provided me with a coaching methodology and framework to empower others and unlock their passions and strengths to get to where they want to go. A methodology that provided a framework to really think about transition.

The Columbia Coaching program not only provided me with the tools, experience, and expertise for my next chapter of life, but it also provided a 10-month opportunity to explore who I was, accept my current reality, define what mattered to me, and decide where I wanted to go. Taking the time to truly understand and incorporate the Columbia Coaching Framework into my coaching practice, as well as into how I looked at my own life, was a game changer.

Context: What's Up?
Content: What Matters?
Conduct: What's next?

Three simple questions that can unlock a lifetime of answers if you let them.

The Columbia Coaching Certification process shed some light, actually a really giant spotlight, on my action orientation and my hesitance to explore the gentler side of things — the emotional side of life.

My Long Island upbringing as the son of a Vietnam-era Infantry Marine turned police officer, coupled with spending almost my entire adult life up to that point as a military officer, did not readily lend itself to the reflective and interpretive areas of the Columbia Coaching framework.

One of the unexpected bonuses of the program was exposure to a wide range of different opinions, perspectives, and insights, which have increased my openness, acceptance, and empathy for others. Once I was encouraged to go into that space, I was amazed at the benefits for me as a person and as a coach, but also for my family members, friends, and clients.

Life Happens For You

The next two stops have some overlap because of why and how they impacted me. In the previous chapter I mentioned exposure being one of the unexpected bonuses of the Columbia Executive Coaching Certification Program. The second bonus was connection to a Mastermind group of other Columbia-trained Executive Coaches who are part of my personal accountability plan to this day.

You may be wondering what a Mastermind group is. A Mastermind is a cohesive group of dedicated peers focused on personal and professional development who share and provide support and perspective to one another through this thing we call life. It's about information, inspiration, collaboration and accountability, and most Masterminds are designed for a specific purpose and target audience.

Besides my Columbia University Coaching Mastermind group, I joined the Iron Sharpens Iron Mastermind program because the concept resonated with me. The lessons that were unearthed from my professional misfortune — the visualization of metal getting stronger from experiencing adversity and hardship — really spoke to me.

The other stop was Fayetteville, Georgia. I have had the opportunity to participate in two cohorts of the Camp Southern Ground Warrior Week program as well as provide ongoing transition coaching support to program alumni. The goal of the Warrior Week program is to help transitioning veterans harness their strength, perseverance, selflessness, sacrifice, integrity, and honor as a springboard to a productive and fulfilling life after service. Not something I wanted to go through, but something I needed to go through in order to sort things out. Camp Southern Ground — the grounds, the staff, and Warrior Week program — is an amazing place for self-discovery.

As a retired military officer, camaraderie and a sense of connection and purpose are an essential part of my identity — something I learned from my ONU experience. As I transitioned from military service, some of that identity was lost due to the realities of post-military life.

The Iron Sharpens Iron Mastermind Group and the Camp Southern Ground Warrior Week Program both provided platforms to interact with and invest in other like-minded individuals who are committed to being better versions of themselves. They also provided some of the camaraderie, connection, and purpose I had been searching for.

The result of both programs has been a renewed sense of spirit, drive, and intentionality to not only better myself but to provide perspective and insight to empower others to get to where they want to go in life.

The Camp Southern Ground Warrior Week program offers a wide range of opportunities such as ax throwing, bow and arrow shooting, and ropes courses. Warrior Week also has a partnership with Creativets whose mission is to empower veterans to heal through the arts and music.

Part of the Warrior Week program curriculum is working with songwriters and fellow participants to develop a song about your transition. Yep, comfort zone departure for sure! However, it was one of the most cathartic experiences I have ever had because it provided an opportunity to dig into a topic I had struggled with for quite some time and from a direction I had never considered before. Here are the words:

HAPPENS FOR YOU

I used to play the victim
Well-versed in "woe is me"
Always wished that it was different
Always wished it didn't have to be

Always focused on the darkness
Never searchin' for the light
I was never open-hearted
Until I realized

       Steel only gets stronger in the flames
       Sometimes you gotta jump right in
       and ride the wave
       Sometimes you feel you're stuck in
       the same place
       And that's just life

But it don't happen to you — it
happens for you

When I breathe the air is sweeter
But sometimes I still break down
But I know my heart is freer
Cause I've finally found

Steel only gets stronger in the flames
Sometimes you gotta jump right in
and ride the wave
Sometimes you feel you're stuck in
the same place
And that's just life
But it don't happen to you — it
happens for you

The key takeaway was the lesson that life
doesn't happen to you, it happens for you.
You've got to realize that the only way you're
going to become stronger, similar to the way

steel gets stronger, is to get tested. That's how you come out better on the other side. You just have to be committed to the process and understand that it's a matter of mindset. Sometimes it is simply saying out loud for you and others to hear, "Heck yeah, that sucked, but how do I move on from it and move in a positive direction? How do I transition to where I want to go?"

I learned a lot about myself during this entire transition process but there were things I didn't fully realize until recently. The way I navigated through my forced transition actually impacted other people because I did not allow them to help or provide the same perspective, insight, or support I would readily provide to someone who mattered to me. Everyone I interacted with thought I was doing okay, but when I reflect back on every wellness area, I struggled and kept it between me and my dog. Being open, vulnerable, and being okay with asking for help is part of any successful transition, be it accidental, forced, or purposeful. Leveraging your personal and professional networks to enable you to get to where you want to go is a necessity for positive action and something I had to learn.

Action: The Program

"The best way to predict your future is to create it."

~ Abraham Lincoln

The key to moving from where you are to where you truly want to go starts with defining what you want and what transition means to you. The answer to that question provides the starting point for self-reflection, exploration, and action.

That's why a picture of Acadia National Park is on the cover — it just makes sense to me. It's a place my wife, one of my key energizers, and I have been together and it is a place to relax, reflect, and recharge. The rocks in the foreground are the essence of adversity. You've got to get through some rough stuff to truly know who you are and where you want to go. The water in the background represents the need for self-reflection, exploration, and action. The lighthouse represents the need to understand and internalize ones' values, priorities, and purpose in order to provide a guiding light for one's expedition. The setting sun epitomizes the cycle of life and the need to live in the present. Finally, Acadia National Park is the home of Cadillac Mountain and, although it only measures 1,530 feet (466 meters) above sea level, it's the highest point along the North Atlantic seaboard and the first place to view sunrise in the United States for almost half the year. It's that energy that will propel us in a positive direction to get us to where we want to go.

What's the Objective?

"Efforts and courage are not enough without purpose and direction."

—John F. Kennedy

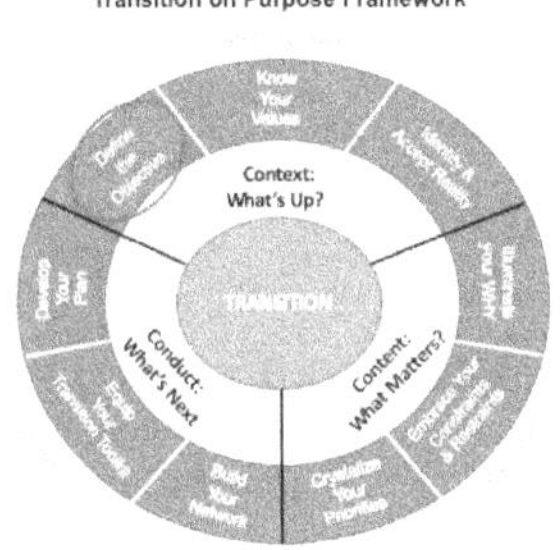

The first step in Transitioning on Purpose is defining the problem. This is a huge part of any operational planning process and is an integral part of any transition plan. Without a defined desired end state, it is hard to build a plan to get there.

New York Yankees legend Yogi Berra once said, "If you don't know where you are going, you'll end up someplace else." As you look at what's next for you, how do you define your transition? Is it simply changing jobs? Changing roles? Is it a career pivot? Is it starting a side hustle to pursue a passion part-time? Is it a lifestyle change? Or maybe a complete career change to pursue a passion full-time? Is it a combination? Taking the time to define your transition provides the objective for your expedition.

The next step in transition planning is defining our success criteria. It is about spending time thinking about what success will look like, feel like, and how we will know we are making the progress we want. If we look at our defined transition objective as an expedition, our success criteria is the destination — the top of that mountain where the view can't be beat — as well as the checkpoints along the way.

Define the Objective

Know Your Values

"Your beliefs become your thoughts, your thoughts become your words, your words become your actions, your actions become your habits, your habits become your values, your values become your destiny."

\- Mahatma Gandhi

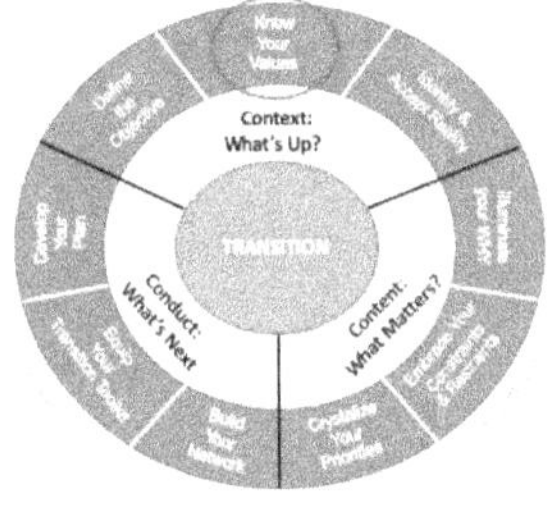

Values are the cornerstone of our personal fulfillment. When we live a life in alignment with our values, we experience the balance and happiness we are looking for. When we live out of synch with our values, we get frustrated, stressed out, and disconnected. When we think about making our defined transition our reality, our values provide the operating area for that decision-making process to happen.

If we view our defined transition as an expedition, then our desired end state — our definition of transition coupled with our established success criteria — provides the destination and checkpoints we need to pass to get there. Our values provide the operational boundaries of our expedition and define who we are — not who we would like to be or think we should be, but who we are in our lives right now. Our character is simply our values in action.

Sometimes we are told what our values are. I certainly was. For 24 years of my life my values were the core values of the Naval Service — Honor, Courage, and Commitment. Organizational values are great to have to guide our professional life, but what about our life decisions? It wasn't until I was forced to think about it that I concluded that while honor, courage, and commitment mattered to me, autonomy, impact, and security mattered more.

I have had the opportunity to participate in a foundational leadership program as a co-facilitator for emerging leaders for the past three years. Exploring one's personal values is an integral part of this program. Imagine getting to think about, identify, define and talk about your personal values for three hours once a month for three years after never really thinking about them for over 24 years. Here is how I think about my personal values now:

Autonomy — To make my own decisions about the work I want to do as well as the people and organizations I want to work with. Autonomy to make decisions about what is best for me and my family and to spend time on the things and with the people that matter to me.

Impact — To spend time and energy on the things that enlighten, empower, and equip others to see and reach their full potential. Impact through providing trusted advice and counsel to enable others to succeed in work and life. Impact by providing others the opportunity for greater knowledge, perspective, and understanding.

Security — Providing the physical, emotional, and financial safety to satisfy the needs of myself and of those who matter to me so we have the freedom to invest our time, energy, intellect, and resources into making the lives of other people better.

What are your top three to five values and how do you define them?

Define the Objective

Know Your Values

Identify and Accept your Reality

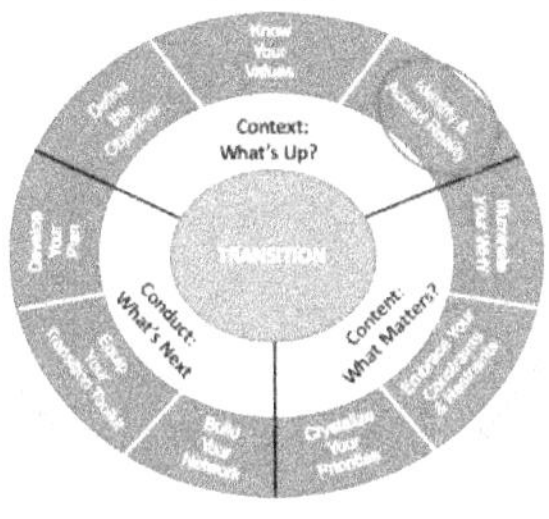

The need for intentional and holistic self-reflection in all aspects of personal wellness cannot be overemphasized because it provides the starting part for this whole transition expedition. Self-reflection requires dedicated time and energy to define the reality of the various aspects of our life so we can explore the options and act where appropriate and warranted. I was introduced to the Co-Active Coaching fulfillment model when I went through the Columbia University Executive Coaching program. The model utilizes eight dimensions to assist in illustrating life balance. I was introduced to The National Wellness Institute's (NWI) Six Dimensions of Wellness Model during my time at Camp Southern Ground. The NWI model also provides an excellent starting point to look at the interdependence of wellness in our lives. I was also introduced to Gallup's *Five Essential Elements of Well-Being* by Tom Rath and Jim Harter when I went through the Gallup Strengths Coaching Certification Course which provides another perspective on personal wellness. After coaching hundreds of emerging leaders, proven mid-level executives, and transitioning military veterans, it made sense to combine some of the concepts. There is a lot of synergy and the combination provides a greater vantage point for overall personal wellness and fulfillment.

While the National Wellness Institute and Gallup define their respective areas of wellness, it is important for us to define what each area of wellness means to us.

With the understanding and appreciation that both the definition and criteria for success can change over time, take a moment to reflect on the key areas below and what the success criteria would be.

Family: How do you define it? How would you rate your relationship with your family? What do you want that relationship to look like?

Significant Other/Romance: What does your

current love life look like? What do you want it to look like in the future?

Friends and Social Health: How are you connecting with the people in your life who provide you with positive energy? How are you limiting your engagement with people in your life who de-energize you?

Fun, Recreation, and Hobbies: How are you spending your time away from work? What are you doing for fun and relaxation? How do you disconnect? What do you miss doing?

Physical Health and Wellness: What are you doing to ensure your function, mobility, and stamina to do the things you want to do? Fitness level? Exercise routine? Health check-up status?

Mental Health and Mindfulness: What are

you doing to maintain your clarity, focus, and creativity? How would you rate your mental toughness? Your grit?

Financial Health: How comfortable are you financially? Emergency fund? Savings? Investments? Debt to income ratio? Credit score?

Intellectual Health: How are you investing in yourself and in your personal development?

Occupational Health: How satisfied are you in your current role at work? What do you dream about doing? What are your interests? What are the options?

Purpose: What's your "why"? How aligned are your actions with your strengths and talents? What are your passions? How are you fulfilling them?

How would you rate yourself in each area of
wellness and what risks, if any, do they
present?

What area(s), if focused on, would have the
greatest impact on your overall wellness?
How?

Define the Objective

Know Your Values

Identify & Accept Your Reality

Illuminate Your "WHY"

"The purpose of life is not to be happy. It is to be useful, to be honorable, to be compassionate, to have it make some difference that you have lived and lived well."

- Ralph Waldo Emerson

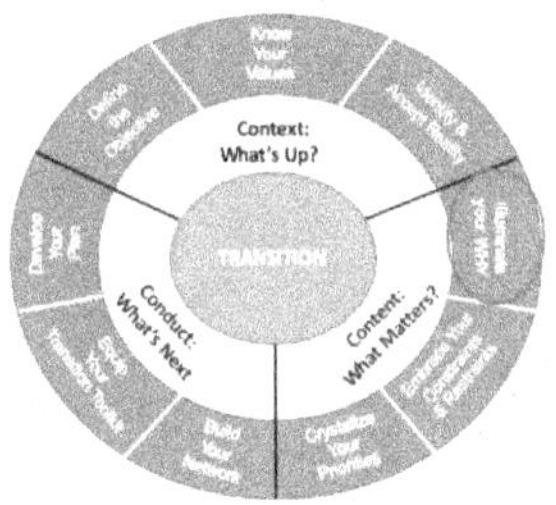

Reflecting on your "WHY" is the next big step because knowing and intentionally living your "WHY" provides the mental toughness and grit necessary to deal with the adversity life will throw at you.

Figuring out your "WHY" is not an easy task. It will take time, energy, and patience, but it is a key component of our personal resilience toolkit, so it's worth it. Your "WHY" will change over time and that is one of the reasons making self-reflection part of your ongoing personal rhythm is so important.

There are three basic questions associated with sorting out your "WHY". First, what are your strengths? What are you good at? You can look for this answer in one of three ways. Quantitively, through online assessments and, as a Gallup certified strengths coach, I highly recommend the Clifton StrengthsFinder assessment. (https://www.gallup.com/access/239204/cliftonstrengths-assessment.aspx). Qualitatively, by asking yourself as well as those in your inner circle. A combination of the previous two by teaming up with a performance coach who can help you make sense of the answers. I did all three and all were helpful in unlocking information and perspectives I hadn't considered before.

The second question is about your passions. What truly energizes you and provides the opportunity to do work that is meaningful to you? Sometimes it's a simple question of do you live to work or work to live? Am I passionate about the work I do? Or do I find my purpose outside of my work life?

The third question is about problem solving. What really matters to you and what will provide energy simply from doing the work? What problems do you want to solve?

Defining your "WHY" is all about fueling our internal desire for change. It's a matter of inspiring the most important participant in your transition — you!

What will allow you to know your life has been well-lived?

Define the Objective

Know Your Values

Identify & Accept Your Reality

Illuminate Your WHY

Embrace Your Constraints and

Restraints

"Boundaries define us. They define what is me and what is not me. A boundary shows me where I end and where someone else begins, leading me to a sense of ownership. Knowing what I am to own and take responsibility for gives me freedom."

- Dr. Henry Cloud

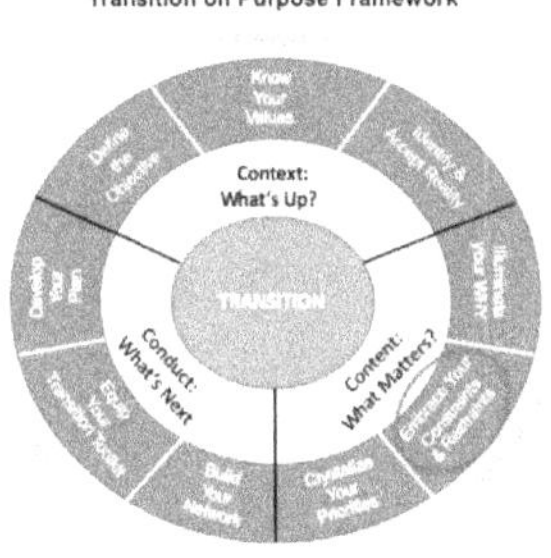

To move forward in a positive direction, it's all about personal change management and allowing our desire for change to outweigh the awareness that change is necessary. A key component of that process is to identify the basics of our human condition — what brings us pain and de-energizes us versus what brings us pleasure and positive energy and enables us to be our best.

The first step is a mindset shift and recognizing that "embracing the suck" each and every day does not have to be our reality. We must harness the power to identify the things we want to do instead of the things we have to do.

The next step is identifying what needs to be in our daily rucksack in terms of Mind, Body, Tribe, and your "Why." Once you have identified what your ideal day needs to look like, do the exact same thing for your ideal week, month, and year.

The final step is establishing a personal defensive perimeter and identifying what and who de-energizes us. We then must put systems, boundaries, and people in place to minimize their occurrence.

What are the energizing activities that need to be part of your daily and weekly routines?

What de-energizes you and what boundaries do you need to put in place to mitigate their impact in the future?

Define the Objective

Know Your Values

Identify & Accept Your Reality

Illuminate Your WHY

Embrace your Constraints & Restraints

Crystalize Your Priorities

"First tell yourself what kind of person you want to be, then do what you have to do. For in nearly every pursuit we see this to be the case. Those in athletic pursuit first choose the sports they want, and then do that work."

- Epictetus

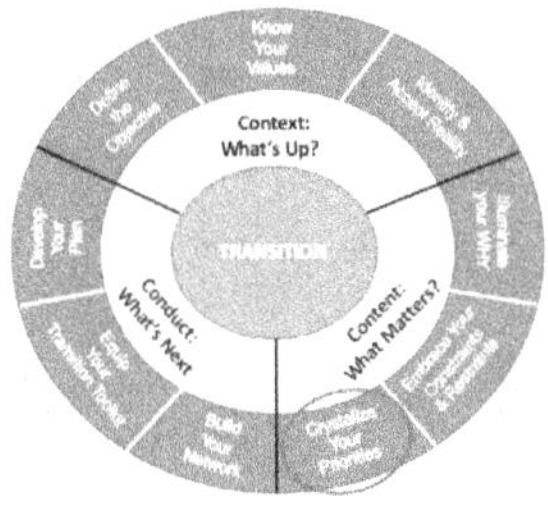

As you plan for your next chapter in life, what needs to be part of your new reality? How can you develop a process that defines "what is" as well as "what needs to be?" Taking the time to identify the gap between the two and what matters most is an integral step in transition planning. Identifying your ideal as well as what you want to prioritize in life is what I commonly refer to as one's personal happiness equation. To get you thinking, some potential priorities could be impactful work, a sense of connection, work/life integration, personal development, mentorship, organizational culture, being part of a dynamic team, and professional growth, just to name a few. What are the variables that support your happiness equation?

Spending time identifying your ideal next chapter of things allows you to say "yes" to what really matters and "no" to the opportunities that do not satisfy your needs.

What are your top 3 priorities as you move into your next chapter?

How will you prioritize what matters to you?

If you don't focus on yourself, no one else will. Take the time to understand who you are and what you want, ask for it, and don't take no for an answer.

Define the Objective

Know Your Values

Identify & Accept Your Reality

Illuminate Your WHY

Embrace your Constraints & Restraints

Crystalize Your Priorities

Build Your Network

"The key is to keep company only with people who uplift you; whose presence calls forth your best."

- Epictetus

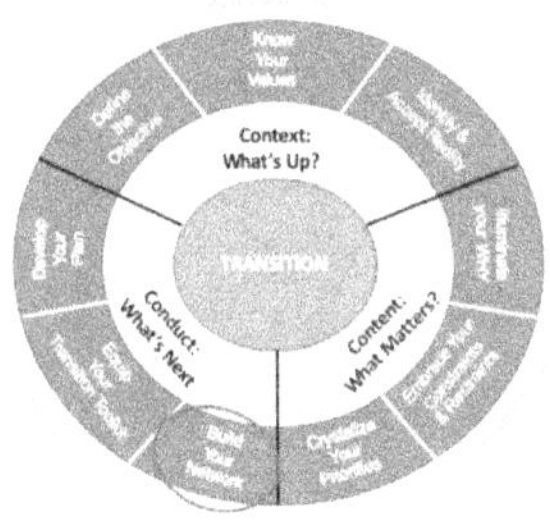

My experience during my time at Operation New Uniform highlighted the need to develop and lean in to my personal network. We participated in an exercise which consisted of reaching out to the five people in our life who have Always Answered Your Call (AAYC), or "ACES". We then connected with their AAYCs and, in a matter

111

of a few weeks, I had 25 new connections from a myriad of different professions and careers and learned about a variety of industries and options. The intent of the exercise was to expand our network while providing the opportunity to gain insight and perspective outside of our normal reality. It's an exercise I recommend for anyone going through transition because of the connections, perspectives, and new relationships that develop from the experience.

This experience made me think about my personal and professional support requirements for my transition expedition. The most glaring requirement was the need for regular connection with the people who were committed to making the lives of other people better. It was a matter of creating an ecosystem, a community of dedicated people who function to uplift and bring out the best in each other. The one recurring nagging question remaincd — how could I create a personal fulfillment ecosystem that, just by its mere presence, positively impacts the lives of those operating within it?

Your Quick Reaction Force (QRF)

"For the strength of the Pack is the Wolf, and the strength of the Wolf is the Pack."

- Rudyard Kipling

As a retired military officer, Quick Reaction Forces (QRFs) were a part of everyday life in the military. What are they and why do we need them in our personal lives? In military circles, a QRF is a military unit capable of rapidly responding to a developing situation with the equipment necessary.

As a career Surface Warfare Officer, life at sea required two types of QRF's — one for security and force protection purposes and the other for firefighting and damage control purposes. Both teams brought different skills, abilities, and expertise to the table. In this case of transition planning and ecosystem development, it's about identifying those five to 10 people in your life you can call on no matter what. These are the people who have the skills, abilities and expertise to give you the insight, perspective, and accountability you need to make good decisions.

Who needs to be part of your personal Quick Reaction Force?

What does a personal QRF look like in action? It depends on what you need and how open you are about your support requirements. It could be a regularly scheduled breakfast at Waffle House to gain perspective and chat about life. It could be someone traveling halfway around the world with their three kids to support you and your family at your retirement celebration. Or it could be someone taking you to a national level HVAC convention just so you can better understand life outside your current reality. It could even be as simple as someone who regularly pushes you outside of your comfort zone just so you can explore different perspectives.

How will you inform your Quick Reaction Force of your support requirements to be most helpful to you and your transition?

Your Tribe

The next step to our Personal Team Building process is developing our Tribe. For me, a Tribe is a group of people who form a community or ecosystem dedicated to positively impacting the lives of those participating in it. While our Tribe includes our QRF, it expands the group to a manageable number of 20 to 30 people because it focuses on more than insight, perspective, and accountability.

What else is our Tribe focused on? A well-functioning Tribe provides a sense of belonging, connection, and a positive recharging energy for its members. Why does it matter? It is a vital part of our personal resilience equation – Mind, Body, Tribe, and Why.

As a lacrosse player from Long Island, I was introduced to Native American culture when I started playing the game. Lacrosse was introduced by the Iroquois Indians in what is now Upstate New York, then spread throughout New England and the mid-Atlantic region and now throughout the entire country.

A successful lacrosse team is comprised of team members specialized in offense, defense, face-offs, or goal-tending who continually focus on mission and team success while competing in the "fastest game on two feet."

The sport of lacrosse and its origins from Native American culture is what got me interested in developing a better understanding of the Tribe concept.

It wasn't until I read Sebastian Junger's book, *Tribe*, many years later during the start of my transition from military service that I truly grasped the concept of what a Tribe meant from both a personal and professional transition perspective. Junger's work explored the lessons from tribal societies' loyalty, the need for belonging, and the human desire for purpose and meaning.

To be successful, a Tribe has to have a true sense of belonging, loyalty, and purpose and it needs to incorporate the wisdom, knowledge, experience, mentorship, technical acumen and expertise of its members in order to move the ecosystem in a positive direction.

Developing our Tribe to enlighten and empower us to take on both the adversity and opportunities life will present is one of our mission essential tasks for transition success.

Who needs to be part of your Tribe?

Thought Leaders?
Mentors?
Catalysts?
Experienced Professionals?
Connectors?
Trusted Colleagues?
Energizers?

Masterminds

As discussed previously, Mastermind groups are small groups of dedicated peers who share and support each other through the challenges of life and leadership. I was first introduced to the concept of Mastermind groups when I read Dr. Joelle Jay's book, *The Inner Edge,* and now Mastermind groups have become part of my new normal. The support from your Mastermind group is personal, practical, and tailored to the needs of each person within the group. The key is to identify what you need and what you are looking for.

As a new executive coach, I was asked to join a Mastermind group of other Columbia University trained executive coaches to meet on a monthly basis to discuss current industry trends, practice and get regular feedback on our coaching skills, and provide communal support for any personal or professional issues the group has. My Columbia Coaching Mastermind Group continues to be extremely beneficial from both a personal and professional perspective because it has kept me up to date on industry trends as well as provided a sense of belonging. It is a geographically diverse group from a variety of different industries and experiences which meets monthly via video chat for an hour. Each session has either a learning session on current coaching industry trends or coaching sessions for participants.

I am also part of the Iron Sharpens Iron (ISI) Mastermind which looks at the personal, professional, and spiritual wellness of group members. It is a 10-member, geographically diverse group from all walks of life which meets weekly via video chat for one hour.

Each week, one or two group members provides a personal topic to dig into and get perspective, recommendations, and accountability on. My ISI Mastermind experience has also been extremely helpful injecting a strong sense of camaraderie and accountability back into my life because of the openness and commitment group members have with one other.

The key ingredients to each of my Mastermind groups are the commitment, dedication, and focus of the group members, coupled with the confidentiality of our conversations. A well-functioning Mastermind group can be a game changer in your transition journey and in life. If you can't find one, create one. You won't regret it.

What can a Mastermind help you solve?

Define the Objective

Know Your Values

Identify & Accept Your Reality

Illuminate Your WHY

Embrace your Constraints &
Restraints

Crystalize Your Priorities

Build Your Network

Equip Your Transition Toolkit

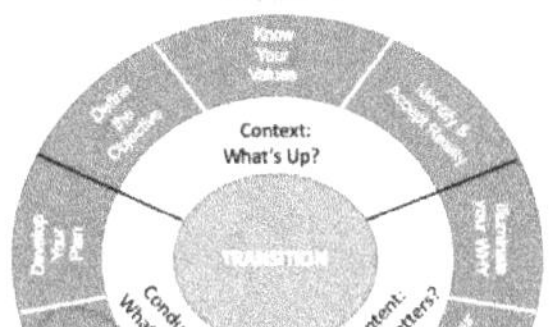

Understanding the connection between emotional intelligence, personal wellness, and our personally defined resilience is a vital component to developing an executable transition plan and living a life with purpose and intent. Based on my experience with transition from the military, numerous geographic transitions, and my coaching experiences over the past few years, the four areas of personal wellness that have the greatest impact on personal and professional resilience are:

Mind: Mental Health and Mindfulness. Our rational thought and the objectivity to provide ourselves with the space needed to think, process, and respond to life by focusing on our locus of control.

What can/do you do to maintain your focus, creativity, and attention?

Body: Physical Health and Wellness. Our ability to promote emotional and mental strength while enabling physical function and mobility.

What type of well-being regimen satisfies your requirements for emotional and mental strength as well as physical function and mobility?

Tribe: Social Health and Wellness. Our ability to develop and maintain our sense of connection, belonging, and purpose.

Who needs to be part of your Tribe?

Why/Purpose: Our spiritual well being. Our ability to understand our strengths, our passions, and the problems we want to solve to fuel our grit and mental toughness.

What are you doing to provide yourself with a powerful source of motivation, determination, and emotional endurance?

Define the Objective

Know Your Values

Identify & Accept Your Reality

Illuminate Your WHY

Embrace your Constraints & Restraints

Crystalize Your Priorities

Build Your Network

Equip your Transition Toolkit

Develop a Plan & Know It'll Change

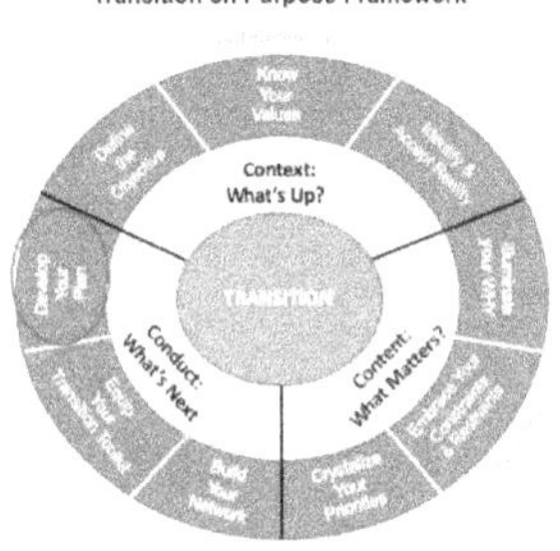

Now that we have an idea of what our transition plan needs to look and feel like, how do we know if it makes sense and will withstand first contact with the outside world? The famous heavyweight boxer Mike Tyson once said, "Everyone has a plan until they get punched in the mouth." So, how can we get past the first punch life throws our way? In military planning, that's the branches and sequels part of the process — knowing what your options are, the cost/benefit analysis of those options, and identifying what the pivot points are. That is what the SEA process is all about — Self-Reflection, Exploration, and Action — in order to search inward, explore outwards, lean towards, and re-engage life.

Military planning principles provide an excellent framework to consider transition plans and personal engagement because it looks at identifying reality, defining success criteria, establishing the operating environment, and developing options and support requirements for success. How can you use military planning principles for your transition planning? Here are some questions to consider:

- How have you defined your transition?

- How have you defined your objective?
- What success criteria is important to you and "Why"?
- How have you determined your operating environment?
- What are your mission essential tasks and how have you planned for them?
- How have you identified your priorities and how will that impact your decision making?
- What are your constraints and restraints? Why?
- Your Network: Your QRF? Your Tribe?
- What are your support requirements to move forward? Who knows about them?

What else is there to think about? Our assumptions. Simply, those things we believe to be true about our current situation or future events in the absence of facts. In military planning, an operational planner must validate planning assumptions as true or false to continue the planning process.

What assumptions have you made about yourself, your reality, and your journey?

Finally, what are the other questions you need to ask yourself about your plan moving forward?

- **Is it Adequate:** Does it accomplish the objective? Does it meet your intent? Does it accomplish all of your needs? Does it meet your criteria for success?

- **Is it Feasible**: Can you accomplish your plan within the established time, space, and resource constraints?

- **Is it Acceptable**: Does it balance cost and risk with the advantage gained? Does it contain unacceptable risks? Personal? Professional? Financial? Does it consider your current and future limitations and constraints?

- **Is it Complete**: Does your plan answer the questions who, what, where, when, how, and why?

Define the Objective

Know Your Values

Identify & Accept Your Reality

Illuminate Your WHY

Embrace your Constraints &
Restraints

Crystalize Your Priorities

Build Your Network

Equip your Transition Toolkit

Develop a Plan & Know it'll
change

The After-Action Report (AAR)

Bottom Line Up Front (BLUF): Adversity is inevitable and is a fact of life. What you decide to do with that adversity is a choice. Life is all about the choices and decisions we make. Transition is a process. Transition is a mindset. You have to decide that your status quo needs to change and then choose the best course of action based on your values, priorities, and what makes sense for your desired end state.

Key Takeaways:

1. Search Inward: Take the time to identify who you are, what matters to you, what you stand for, what you want, and why. Define your reality, identify your ideal, and develop a plan to get there. The only way to get what you want is to actually know what you want, and get after it!

2. Explore Outwards: Identify the opportunities that speak to your strengths. Follow your passions and your sense of purpose. Work on the things that matter to you and will make the difference you are

looking for. The only way to change the world is to start in your own backyard.

3. Lean Towards: Develop your personal QRF and your Tribe with people who will lift you up and continue to make you better each and every day. Connect with them, trust them, and embrace life with them.

4. Act Now: Re-engage! Life is all about what we make of it and you only get one. Take risks, fail often, and seek to be outside your comfort zone because that's where growth happens. Be fearless and open to new experiences and ideas. Be vulnerable. Be humble. Be you.

Ever tried. Ever failed. No matter. Try again. Fail again. Fail better.

- Samuel Beckett

Thank you

Thank you to my TRIBE for supporting me, encouraging me and challenging me to be better each and every day!

Always remember there are only three basic questions to answer when it comes to Transition.

- What's up? Where are you now and where do you want to go? That's reality and the objective.
- What matters? Why do you want to get there? That's the motivation.
- What's next? That's the plan and those who are part of it.

What are the nine secrets to get us there?

Define the Objective

Know Your Values

Identify & Accept Your Reality

Illuminate Your WHY

Embrace your Constraints &
Restraints

Crystalize Your Priorities

Build Your Network

Equip your Transition Toolkit

Develop a Plan & Know it'll change

The Man in the Arena

"It is not the critic who counts; not the man who points out how the strong man stumbles, or where the doer of deeds could have done them better. The credit belongs to the man who is actually in the arena, whose face is marred by dust and sweat and blood; who strives valiantly; who errs, who comes short again and again, because there is no effort without error and shortcoming; but who does actually strive to do the deeds; who knows great enthusiasms, the great devotions; who spends himself in a worthy cause; who at best, knows in the end the triumph of high achievement, and who at the worst, if he fails, at least fails while daring greatly, so that his place shall never be with those cold and timid souls who neither know victory nor defeat."

- President Theodore Roosevelt, France, 1910 – part of his speech on Citizenship in the Republic

LET'S CONNECT

If you'd like to continue the conversation about transitioning on purpose and truly pursuing what really matters to you, or to learn more about other areas of interest, you can contact Dennis at:

Email: Dennis.Volpe@LRI.com

Online: https://transitiononpurpose.com/

LinkedIn: https://www.linkedin.com/in/djvolpe/

To bring Transition on Purpose, Emotional Intelligence, Resilience, Risk Management, Decision-Making, or Emerging Leader Development to your organization – as Microsoft, Citi, United Technologies, Precision Castparts Corporation, the Federal Bureau of Prisons, the Florida Army National Guard, and Camp Southern Ground have – please go to:

www.transitiononpurpose.com/speaking.

Thanks for reaching out!